Respecting DIVERSITY

Written by Anastasia Suen

Content Consultant
Taylor K. Barton, LPC
School Counselor

Rourke
Educational Media

rourkeeducationalmedia.com

Scan for Related Titles
and Teacher Resources

www.rourkeeducationalmedia.com

PHOTO CREDITS: Cover: ©Shaun Lowe; Page 4: © GlobalStock; Page 5: © Jani Bryson; Page 6, 7: © Aldo Murillo; Page 8, 14: © kali9; Page 9: © Blend Images; Page 10: © Izabela Habur; Page 11: © Denis Kuvaev; Page 13: © EHStock; Page 15: © londoneye; Page 16: © Johnny Greig; Page 17: © Elena Elisseeva; Page 18: © Sheryl Griffin; Page 19: © Lucky Business; Page 21: © Jani Bryson; Page 22: © GlobalStock

Edited by Precious McKenzie

Cover and Interior Design by Tara Raymo

Library of Congress PCN Data

Respecting Diversity / Anastasia Suen
(Social Skills)
ISBN 978-1-62169-911-8 (hard cover) (alk. paper)
ISBN 978-1-62169-806-7 (soft cover)
ISBN 978-1-62717-017-8 (e-Book)
Library of Congress Control Number: 2013937306

Rourke Educational Media
Printed in the United States of America,
North Mankato, Minnesota

Also Available as:

ROURKE'S
e-Books

Rourke
Educational Media

rourkeeducationalmedia.com

customersevice@rourkeeducationalmedia.com • PO Box 643328 Vero Beach, Florida 32964

TABLE OF CONTENTS

WHAT IS DIVERSITY?

Diversity is a fancy word. We use it when things are different. Plants can be diverse. There are many plants in the world but they are each different from one another. Each plant is **unique**, or special in its own way.

There is diversity in every area of the natural world.

People can be diverse, too. Yes, people are alike in many ways, but they are also different. The way people look on the outside can be different. The skin we live in comes in many different colors.

Our **heritage** can be seen in our skin, but that is not all that we are. We are more than what we look like on the outside.

Despite our external differences, we can work together as a team.

The way people think can be different, too. Not everyone has the same **beliefs**. We don't all eat the same food or play the same games. We don't all practice the same religion or believe in the same political party.

Every **culture** has **traditions** that we can share.

Everyone is different in some way, even you. It's okay to be different. Diversity is a fact of life. It's how you act when you encounter these differences.

Can you look beyond the disability and see the person?

When you meet someone who has a disability, what do you do? Do you stare? Do you ask what is wrong? Do you focus on the differences? Is that person's disability all that you see?

Don't let someone's disability interrupt a friendship.

JUMPING TO JUDGMENT

It's very easy to see differences on the outside. Unfortunately, we often make **judgments** based on what we see. We judge before we know all the facts. That's **prejudice**.

When a new student comes to class, it's easy to look at the outside and judge. When that person is not the same as you, it's easy to say that they are bad. But that judgment was made without all of the facts.

How would you feel if everyone was staring at you?

13

Playing together is a good way to get to know someone.

When you meet someone new, don't make a judgment. Have an open mind and welcome them instead. Take time to get to know that person for yourself.

Sharing a meal together gives you time to talk and get to know one another.

You may have a lot in **common** with people who look different than you on the outside. You may find out that the new student likes the same things that you do. You may play the same sports. You may eat the same food at lunch.

Music is a universal language we all share.

You may listen to the same music and go to the same movies. You may have the same favorite subjects in school. You won't know what you have in common unless you ask. Don't miss out on the chance to make a new friend!

DEALING WITH DIFFERENCES

Sometimes it feels like life would be so much easier if everyone was just like you! It's not easy to accept that everyone is different.

Have you ever told someone, "Why can't you do it my way?" Did they say the same thing back to you?

Just because you live together doesn't mean you think the same way. Even brothers and sisters have their own ideas.

But you know that even at home that's just not the way it works. Even people in the same family like to do things differently.

No one likes to be told what to do.

It's almost impossible to make other people change. They don't want to do what you say, and they don't want you to tell them what they should do. Well, to be honest, you don't like it when they tell you what to do either!

How do you deal with differences? The answer is **tolerance**. You can decide to let other people be who they are. You can decide to accept the fact that everyone is different. Not everyone looks or thinks the same and that's okay.

You don't have to judge everyone around you. You don't have to try and change other people either. The truth is, the only person you can change is yourself.

You don't have to change other people, but that doesn't mean you can't change the world. You can work with others to help make our world a better place for everyone.

Respecting diversity means respecting other people, whether they are like you or not. It also means that you respect yourself and your own differences. Accepting diversity means understanding that you are unique, too. There is no one else exactly like you.

GLOSSARY

beliefs (bi-LEEFS): ideas that we support

common (KOM-uhn): shared by more than one person

culture (KUHL-chur): the way of life for a group of people

diversity (di-VUR-suh-tee): a variety of choices

heritage (HER-uh-tij): traditions passed from one generation to the next

judgments (JUHJ-muhntss): opinions of something or someone

prejudice (PREJ-uh-diss): a fixed or unreasonable opinion formed without the facts

tolerance (TOL-ur-uhnss): the willingness to respect how others think and act

traditions (truh-DISH-uhns): ways of doing things that is handed down from one generation to the next

unique (yoo-NEEK): one of a kind

INDEX

WEBSITES TO VISIT

www.tolerance.org/lesson/anti-racism-activity-sneetches

www.tolerance.org/lesson/why-frogs-and-snakes-never-play-together

www.tolerance.org/activity/cooperative-comics

ABOUT THE AUTHOR

Anastasia Suen lives with her family in Plano, Texas. She has taught kindergarten to college and worked with wonderful students from all over the world.

Meet The Author!
www.meetREMauthors.com